For Marilyn, Burt, Eric, Neil,
Sheila and Bruce.

# ACKNOWLEDGMENTS

*The Smiley Dictionary* is the result of many years of research and computation. Obviously, a book of this import and magnitude would never be possible without the input and assistance of many people.

Michael Cader provided the initial idea that started me on this trail, and Ted Nace has been a supportive and insightful editor. Robert Gehorsam, Steve Case and Mary Kay Fenner have helped me a great deal, both personally and with their tremendous efforts to make bulletin boards a reality.

As always, thanks to Lucy and Helene, and to the excellent SGP staff: Margery Mandell, Ellen Kenny, Margaret Talcott, Lisa DiMona, and Julie Maner.

# FOREWORD

Conversing online is a sweet, simple glimpse into the power of virtual reality. With just a modem and a screen and tiny digital bits of information, it is amazing how clearly one can visualize the personalities of the people you chat with online. The cynic who leans up against the wall with his arms crossed, the cheerleader who spends most of her time greeting people and hugging them hello, the sophisticated flirt who knows how to liven up a room and get everyone involved and animated, the bore whom most others try to ignore, the stud who's looking for a one-night stand, the activist who wants to further a cause. In a room full of people, none of whom you can see, how do you get these impressions? If we no longer have our visual clues that key us in to people's characters, what is it that comes across?

We all have our little idiosyncracies, our standards, that we instinctively lock into when we meet someone new. Online, we still use some sort of standards—they just change form. For instance, I find I don't flirt with guys who put their apostrophes in the wrong place or who scatter ellipses throughout their sentences. It's like greasy hair or a bad smell. But a witty phrase or a well-shaped sentence wins my heart. Which is reality? Who cares?

Since "words is all we got," people have become very creative with typographic characters, words and beyond, to clue us in to feelings and innuendos and sarcasm and jokes. Smileys are one of these creative forms. The first time you see one online, it seems a little corny. But it doesn't take long to get the fact that they serve a bigger purpose than just being cute. The first time you're offended by a **:-P** on the screen, you get it. When someone you have a crush on signs a letter with a **:-*** , you get it. And when you see a bad joke and respond with a **:-/** , you're in.

:-)

Robin Williams
author of
*The Mac is not a typewriter*
&
*The Little Mac Book*

# PREFACE

The Smiley marks a major milestone in non-verbal communication. Until the advent of the smiley, otherwise known as an emoticon, individuals using electronic communication had no way to indicate subtle mood changes. They couldn't tell jokes, use irony, slip in a pun or become bitingly sarcastic.

Properly used, a smiley can spice up virtually any form of written communication. Now you can say, "Boy, isn't he intelligent :-)" and make it quite clear that you think the subject is an idiot.

Of course, the user has to be certain that the recipient is aware of the many smiley dialects, else the potential for total confusion.

*The Smiley Dictionary* is divided into several chapters, categorizing smileys into several arbitrary groups. An index at the end of the book makes it easy for you to find your favorites.

After an overview of the Classic Smileys, you'll find an in-depth look at Character Smileys. These smileys take a minute or two to "get." Then, suddenly, the frisson of understanding, the gestalt of the whole shebang becomes clear and you understand the message.

Limited in their day-to-day usefulness, Character Smileys are fun to create and really cool.

Celebrities are considered by many to be the highest expression of the smiley art form. Using nothing but standard keyboard characters, you can evoke politicians, religious leaders and even cartoon characters.

Celebrity Smileys are certainly the least useful of all smileys, and this adds to their panache. Their only function in a letter is to say, "Look at me! I'm a celebrity!"

Next, you'll find Nasty Smileys and Challenging Smileys. Both offer you the chance to really express yourself, while annoying or perplexing the recipient.

Finally, take a look at the most common Non-Smiley Smileys. These are special symbols used to capture some of the same meanings as smileys—but without the humor.

# CONTENTS

# CLASSIC SMILEYS

Your basic smiley

Midget smiley

Winking happy smiley

Left-handed smiley

Smiley big-face

Very unhappy smiley

Wry and winking smiley

"Omigod!!"

Winking smiley

My lips are sealed

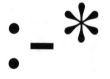

Kiss

Skeptical smiley

Sarcastic smiley

Screaming smiley

Said with a smile

Shouting smiley

:-X

A big wet kiss!

:-\

Undecided smiley

Smiley blockhead

Crying smiley

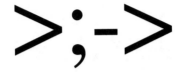

A very lewd remark was just made

Smirking smiley

# CHARACTERS

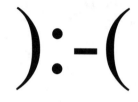

Smiley after staring at a screen for 15
hours straight

)•-(

Nordic smiley

Lucy my pet dog smiley

Tongue-tied

# 8:-)

Little girl smiley

# :-)8<

Big girl smiley

:-0

Talkative smiley

:-6

Smiley after eating
something spicy

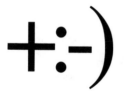

Priest smiley

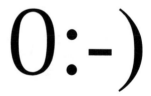

Angel smiley

Walrus smiley

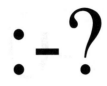

Smiley smokes a pipe

Bucktoothed vampire

Smoking smiley

:-}X

Bow tie-wearing smiley

:-[

Vampire smiley

:-a

Smiley touching
her tongue to her nose

:-{

Mustache

:-{ }

Smiley wears lipstick

:-©

Entertainment-lawyer smiley

Lawyer smiley

Confused Spanish smiley

15

:-8——

Dragonfly smiley

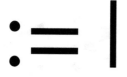

Baboon smiley

Gleep. A friendly midget smiley
who will gladly be your friend.

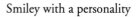

Smiley with a personality

Dunce smiley

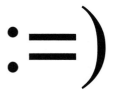

Orangutan smiley

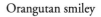

Devilish smiley

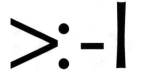

Klingon smiley

@:-)

Smiley wearing a turban

@:-}

Smiley just back from the hairdresser

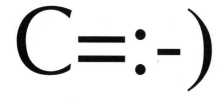

Chef smiley

Little kid
with a propeller beanie

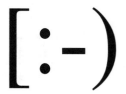

Smiley wearing a Walkman

Robot smiley

{:-)

Smiley wears a toupee

Hepcat smiley

|~(

"Someone just busted my nose"

Pointy-nosed smiley in an updraft

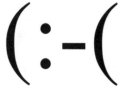

Smoking smiley

The saddest smiley

:-(=)

Bucktooth smiley

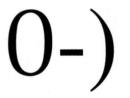

Message from cyclops

:-3

Handlebar mustache smiley

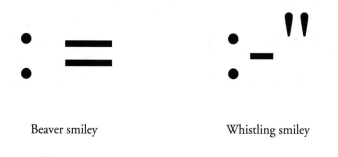

Beaver smiley

Whistling smiley

Pirate smiley

Black eye

d:-)

Baseball-player smiley

:8)

Piggish smiley

Smirking smiley

):-)

Impish smiley

Fan of REM and U2                    Extremely bignosed smiley

# CELEBRITIES

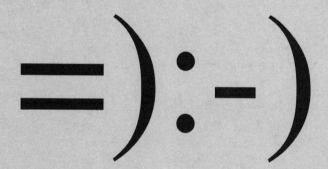

Popeye's kid

David Letterman

Uncle Sam

Shirley Temple with a dimple

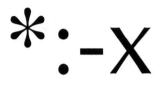

Chuckles the (dead) Clown

Abraham Lincoln

Santa Claus

+O<:-)

The Pope

≈8<: )x

Zippy the Pinhead

(8-o

It's Mr. Bill!

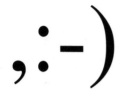

Ronald Reagan (version 1)

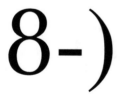

Stevie Wonder

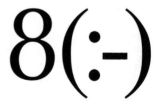

Ronald Reagan (version 2)

Mickey Mouse

# 8(:-)8

Annette Funicello

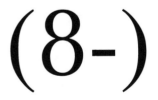

Mark Spitz

# 8-]

Dan Quayle

:-)-!<

Hank Aaron

*<:o)

Bozo the Clown

34

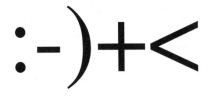

Gumby

Groucho

Geordie LaForge

Moshe Dayan

Catfish Hunter

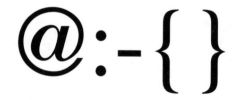

Tammy Faye Baker

# @#$!

Howard Stern

Colonel Klink

([(

Robocop

c|:-=)

Charlie Chaplin

3:*)

Rudolph the red-nosed reindeer

4:-)

George Washington

# NASTY

:-(*)

That comment made me sick

&-|

That made me cry

:-e

Disappointed smiley

:'(

Smiley is having a
pity party in your honor

42

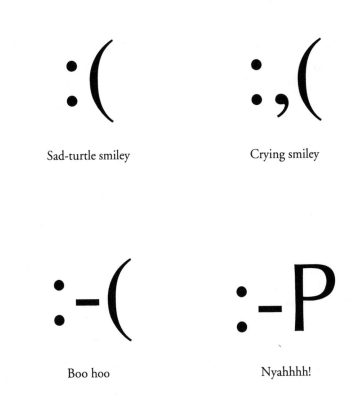

Sad-turtle smiley

Crying smiley

Boo hoo

Nyahhhh!

43

:-S

What you say makes no sense

Un-smiley blockhead

:-C

Real unhappy smiley

Smiley raspberry

:-t

Pouting smiley

:-w

Speak with forked tongue

:-§

One heck of a cold sore!

X-(

You are brain dead

|-O

Smiley is yawning/snoring

|:-O

Flattop loudmouth smiley

~~:-(

So stupid, smoke is coming
out of your brain

46

$-)

Yuppie scum!

Foot in mouth

You lie like Pinnochio

47

# CHALLENGING

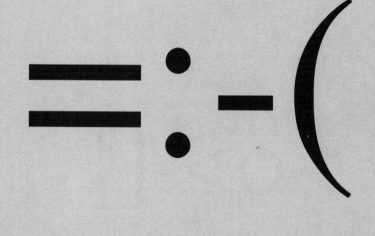

|-o

Bored smiley

)O-)

Scuba smiley

:-o>-[]

Agape American tourist with camera

{@:-)}

Genie in a bottle

0-)    =:-)

Smiley after smoking a banana        Smiley is a punk rocker

=:-(

Real punk rockers don't smile

3:[

Pit Bull smiley

8<:-)

Smiley is a wizard

# 8-#

Dead smiley

# 8:-)

Glasses on forehead

Drunk smiley

Smiley wears braces

:-$

Smiley with his
mouth wired shut

:-F

Bucktoothed vampire
with one tooth missing

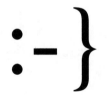

Toasted, inebriated,
sloshed smiley

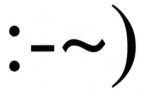

Runny nose

:-¢

Accountant smiley

:-£

English banker

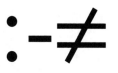

Don't say anything

Wishy-washy smiley

:-)+≈

Big headed skiier

Open-mouthed kiss

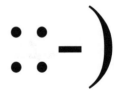

Smiley wears glasses

:^D

Talk show smiley

<|||:|||)

Smiley lives in a multi-story apartment building

Anorexic smiley

Genie smiley

Taoist monk

Smiley is very hot

d8=

Your pet beaver is wearing
goggles and a hard hat.

Message from a thief: Hands up!

59

Smiley with a fever

Biting one's tongue

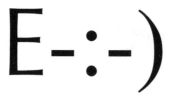

Ham radio operator smiley

Haight Ashbury smiley

<<<<:-)

Hat salesman

:-)-O

Smiley doctor with a stethoscope

)8-)

Smiley is ready to party all night

}:-(

Toupee in an updraft

<||:-)

Smiley likes to sail

# NON-SMILEYS

<g>

Grin

<s>

Sigh

<|>

Laugh

<i>

Irony

&lt;jk&gt;

Just kidding

• • •

Back in a sec

&lt; &gt;

No comment

\|//

Live long and prosper

# AN HISTORICAL NOTE

During the heart of the Cold War, President Kennedy signed Secret Executive Order #345, creating the Institute for Non-Verbal Written Communication. (INVWC). The INVWC was created to address two pressing needs:

1. American messages were being intercepted by Cuban forces, thus nullifying our advantage in the clandestine world of secret messages.

2. We had no way of determining if messages received were in fact genuine.

The crisis that caused this panic is well known to most—The Bay of Piglets. Using information uncovered through the Freedom of Information Act, we have determined that the incident was caused by an imposter.

Apparently, a Soviet spy named Victor Balanesvsky was able to crack the infamous "baseball" code—a code that had been in use for more than thirty years. By asking trivia questions about the New York Yankees, sentries were able to determine who was really on our side.

After buying a copy of *The Baseball Almanac*, Mr. Balanevsky was able to answer all questions about the Yankees. The false messages he sent created chaos throughout the halls of the Pentagon, nearly causing a war.

Research by the Rand Corporation determined that an "unbreakable" code could be created by using characters on an ordinary keyboard. By using references to cultural artifacts, the cryptographers could ensure that only loyal Americans would be able to decode each message. For example, a New Yorker might interpret :-) to be a smiling face, while a typical Muscovite would see a pickled cabbage. Dubbed "Emoticons," they became an instant hit among scientists.

After more than two years of extensive research, conducted by leading physicists, linguists, philosophers and cartoonists, the basic dictionary of smileys was created. Some of the people involved in the project included Stephen Hawking, Keith Haring, Richard Feynman, Guy Kawasaki (he's involved in everything), Steven Seagal and Albert Einstein.

Known as the Pink Book, only one copy of this dictionary was created. It was so secret, no one had sufficient clearance to read it. In fact, the man who printed it was killed so that he wouldn't be able to share his secret. The book was bound in pink magnesium covers, then burned, placed in a trunk and buried at the bottom of the Atlantic.

Unfortunately, no one kept a backup, and the research was lost to the world. Or so we thought.

Ten years ago, Seth Godin, M.R.A., a noted researcher at Brown University, unearthed the first hint that the Emoticon Project had ever taken place. Beginning with the tiniest hint of a notion, he pursued the work vigorously, taking a sabbatical and devoting himself full-time to unearthing any clues as to what had happened.

Just as he was about to give up, he came across his breakthrough. Two teenagers necking on a beach in Florida found a mysterious trunk. After alerting the Air Force, the local police remembered an odd professor who'd been poking around. They called Godin.

The rest is history. The Pink Book hadn't been burned as thoroughly as the researchers had intended, and Godin was able to use advanced chemical chromatography to recreate most of the smileys contained therein.

He immediately recreated the INVWC and began his life's work—spreading the message behind the smileys. Using many aliases, operating under the stealth of night, he infiltrated CompuServe, the Internet, America Online, Prodigy, and even local bulletin boards.

What you hold in your hands today represents the life work of many talented people. On a personal note, The Emoticon Project was an important part of my life, and I'm pleased that the work we did has survived. Enjoy it.

General Roger Smoothy, USAF, Ret.

# THE SEARCH CONTINUES . . .

The Institute continues the search for exciting, unique and clever smileys. If you discover a really cool smiley, send it along. We'd love to hear from you.

We'll include the very best smileys in the next volume of *The Smiley Dictionary*.

Send your contributions to:

THE INSTITUTE FOR NON-VERBAL WRITTEN COMMUNICATION
SETHWOOD@AOL.COM via the Internet
BBBT98A via Prodigy

## VALUABLE COUPON

# SAVE $5 ON
# YOUR ACCOUNT ON
# *COMPUSERVE*

This certificate is worth $5 in CompuServe connect time.
Enclose this coupon with your bill. Only one coupon per
customer. Coupon is non-transferable. Void where
prohibited.

NAME: _____

ADDRESS: _____

CITY, STATE, ZIP: _____

CompuServe User ID: _____

## VALUABLE COUPON

# TRY *AMERICA ONLINE* FREE!

Send in this coupon, and we will send you a free America Online starter kit, and some free time to try America's Most Exciting Online Service.

NAME: _____

ADDRESS: _____

CITY, STATE, ZIP: _____

Which version of the America Online software would you like?
[ ] Windows    [ ] DOS    [ ] Macintosh

Disk Size: [ ] 3.5 inch    [ ] 5.25 inch

Send to: AOL, Free Starter Kit, 8619 Westwood Center Drive, Vienna VA 22182

# ALPHABETICAL INDEX

# ALPHABETICAL INDEX

# ALPHABETICAL INDEX

# ALPHABETICAL INDEX

## SMILEY INDEX

# SMILEY INDEX

# SMILEY INDEX

# SMILEY INDEX

# THE
# SMILEY
# DICTIONARY

## Seth Godin

Foreword by
Robin Williams

Peachpit Press

# THE SMILEY DICTIONARY
Seth Godin

Peachpit Press, Inc.
2414 Sixth Street
Berkeley, California 94710
(800) 283.9444
(510) 548.4393
(510) 548.5991 fax

ISBN 1-56609-008-3
0 9 8 7 6 5 4 3 2
Printed and bound in the United States of America.